Safety First!

Safety around Fire

by Lucia Raatma

Consultant:
F. C. (Fred) Windisch
Chairman, Volunteer Chief Officers Section
International Association of Fire Chiefs

Bridgestone Books

an imprint of Capstone Press
Mankato, Minnesota

Bridgestone Books are published by Capstone Press
818 North Willow Street, Mankato, Minnesota 56001
http://www.capstone-press.com

Library of Congress Cataloging-in-Publication Data
Raatma, Lucia.
    Safety around fire/by Lucia Raatma.
    p. cm.—(Safety first!)
    Includes bibliographical references and index.
    Summary: Describes different sources of fire and how to stay safe around
fires both indoors and outside.
    ISBN 0-7368-0190-1
    1. Fire prevention—Juvenile literature. 2. Fire—Juvenile literature. [1. Fire
prevention. 2. Safety.] I. Title. II. Series: Raatma, Lucia. Safety first.
TH9148.R33 1999
628.9'22—dc21
                                                                    98-44689
                                                                        CIP
                                                                         AC

Editorial Credits
Rebecca Glaser, editor; Steve Christensen, cover designer and illustrator;
    Kimberly Danger, photo researcher

Photo Credits
David F. Clobes, 6, 8, 10, 14, 16, 20
International Stock/Dusty Willison, cover
Mary E. Messenger, 18
Photo Network/K. L. Giese, 12
Photophile/Mark M. Walker, 4

Table of Contents

Good Fires and Bad Fires

Fire can be good or bad. Good fires cook food and warm you. Good fires are controlled. But fires can get out of control. These bad fires can hurt you. You must be careful around all fires.

Preventing Fire

Flammable objects such as clothing and newspapers catch fire easily. Keep flammable objects away from space heaters, stoves, and other heat sources. Help an adult check for any flammable objects in your home. Move these objects away from heat sources.

flammable
able to catch fire easily

Matches and Lighters

Adults use matches and lighters to start good fires. Never play with matches or lighters. You could start a fire by accident. Give any matches and lighters you find to an adult.

accident
something not planned
that often hurts people

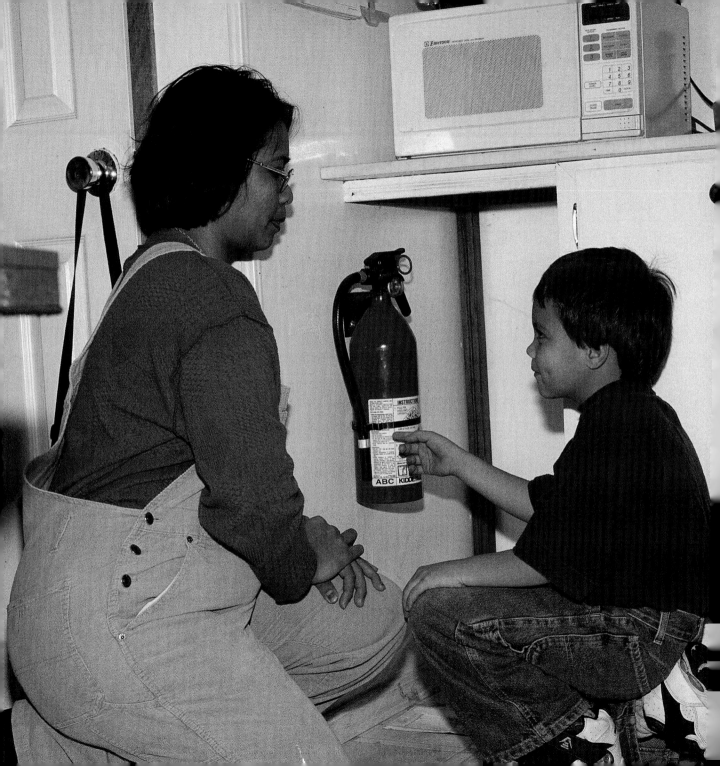

Fire Safety in the Kitchen

Kitchens have hot stoves and ovens that can hurt you. Stay away from hot stove burners. Never put toys or other flammable objects in the oven. Cooking can sometimes cause fires. Ask an adult to keep a fire extinguisher in your kitchen.

fire extinguisher

a holder with water or safe chemicals inside it; adults may use fire extinguishers to put out small fires.

11

Cooking Outside

You need to be careful around campfires and outdoor grills. Do not go too close to these fires. Adults should do the cooking. Never throw objects into a fire. And never add lighter fluid to a fire. The fire will become much larger. It could get out of control.

lighter fluid

a flammable liquid used to light charcoal in grills; only adults should use lighter fluid.

Fire Safety with Decorations

Do not let a bad fire start at a special occasion. Keep holiday decorations away from candles and fireplaces. Be careful when blowing out birthday candles. Keep your hair away from the candle flames.

Stop, Drop, and Roll

Fire can hurt you and may scare you. But never run if fire touches you. Instead, stop what you are doing. Drop to the ground. Cover your face with your hands. Roll on the ground until the fire is out. Then find an adult to help you.

Smoke Alarms

Smoke alarms sound when they sense smoke. The alarm warns you to get out fast. Ask an adult to put a smoke alarm on each level of your home. Adults should test each smoke alarm once a month. Adults should replace smoke alarm batteries twice each year.

battery

a small container that provides electricity; some smoke alarms need batteries for power.

19

Prepare for Escape

Your family should prepare to escape quickly from fire. Plan an escape route. Everyone should know two ways to escape from each room. Plan to use a window or another escape path if fire blocks a door. Crawl low under smoke as you escape.

Hands On: Plan an Escape Route

You and your family should know what to do if there is a fire. Meet with your family members to plan an escape route.

What You Need
Paper
Black marker
Red marker
The members of your family

What You Do
1. Use the black marker to draw a map of your home.
2. Circle windows and doors on the map with the red marker. These are exits. Find two exits for every room.
3. Draw the best way to get out of each room.
4. Everyone should learn two ways out of each room.
5. Choose a place where your family will meet outside. Mark your meeting place on the map.
6. Practice a fire drill.

Words to Know

battery (BAT-uh-ree)—a small container that provides electricity; some smoke alarms need batteries for power.

escape route (ess-KAPE ROOT)—a planned way to leave your home

fire extinguisher (FIRE ek-STING-gwish-ur)—a holder with water or safe chemicals inside it; adults may use fire extinguishers to put out small fires.

flammable (FLAM-uh-buhl)—able to burn

smoke alarm (SMOHK uh-LARM)—a machine that senses smoke and warns people by making a loud sound

Read More

Loewen, Nancy. *Fire Safety.* Plymouth, Minn.: Child's World, 1997.

Raatma, Lucia. *Home Fire Drills.* Fire Safety. Mankato, Minn.: Bridgestone Books, 1999.

Internet Sites

Fire Safety ABCs—The Police Notebook
http://www.ou.edu/oupd/fireprim.htm
Sparky's Home Page
http://www.sparky.org
USFA (U.S. Fire Administration) Kids Homepage
http://www.usfa.fema.gov/kids

Index